HOW TO CREATE PICTURE BOOKS

written and illustrated

by Mike Artell

This book is for
young authors and illustrators everywhere . . .
and for the wonderful people who teach them.

Publisher: Roberta Suid
Editor: Murray Suid
Design: David Hale
Copy Editor: Carol Whiteley
Production: Santa Monica Press
Consultant: Sue Krumbein

Other Monday Morning publications of related interest are:
Book Factory MM 979
More Book Factory MM 1935
Picture Book Factory MM 1933
Storybooks Teach Writing MM 1990

ISBN 1-878279-62-9

CONTENTS

INTRODUCTION

We all have stories to tell. One of the most exciting ways to tell them is by combining pictures and words. Examples include many of the world's best-loved books, such as *Goodnight Moon* and *The Tale of Peter Rabbit*.

HOW TO CREATE PICTURE BOOKS teaches the secrets for producing this delightful kind of literature. Activities take various forms: writing practices, drawing experiments, checklists, library scavenger hunts, and publishing real books. Pages are filled with models and helpful hints.

The book has six parts:

- **Take the First Step** explores what makes picture books so special.

- **Get Ideas** suggests ways for finding subjects. Tips range from people watching to inventing wild characters.

- **Write Your Story** covers plotting, scenes, outlining, drafting, and revising.

- **Design the Book** reveals secrets for planning pages that have eye appeal.

- **Create the Art** focuses on drawing, color, special effects, borders, and viewpoint.

- **Publish the Book** explains how to bring all the parts together. Topics include creating covers, lettering, and binding pages. There is also advice about sharing and evaluating the finished book.

The **Resources** section includes a list of model picture books, plus guides to special art techniques.

How to Use This Book

One option is to try some or all the practices—keeping them together in a journal or portfolio— and then, with skills sharpened, work on a real book. Another approach is to launch an actual book project from the very first day, and use the index to locate help on solving specific problems.

There's no one right way to be creative. What matters is hard work and imagination. Hopefully, the results will be picture books that are worth sharing with friends, and that will be as much fun to read years from now as they are today.

Note for Teachers

These materials can be used by students working alone or in small groups. For whole-class activities, such as getting involved in Young Authors Conferences and taking field trips, see pages 78 and 79.

PART 1

TAKE THE FIRST STEP

GO ON A BOOK HUNT

Just as there are many kinds of games, movies, and music, there are many kinds of picture books. Which kind will you want to write? To answer that question, you need to know your choices.

Try this: *Read many kinds of picture books. Some of the most popular types are listed in the box. Your teacher or librarian can help you find examples. In your writer's journal, make a note of the kind of picture book you like best.*

A Few Kinds of Picture Books

- ABC books
- Adventure stories
- Animal books
- Bedtime stories
- Biographies
- Dream stories

- Folk tales
- How-to-do-it books
- Humorous stories
- Nature stories
- Real-life stories
- Scary tales

Bonus: *Visit a bookstore that sells picture books. What kinds of books are on display? You might ask the store's manager to point out books that kids and parents enjoy reading. Ask to look at award-winning books. Can you figure out what makes these books special?*

HOW TO CREATE PICTURE BOOKS

TAKE A PICTURE BOOK QUIZ

Before you write picture books, it helps to learn what you can about them. Here's a chance for you to find out how much you already know about this important kind of literature.

Try this: *Think about the statements below. Then decide if you agree or disagree.*

1. Picture books are "baby" books.

2. All picture books have words.

3. Picture books are always about imaginary characters, such as talking bunnies.

4. Some picture books have rhyming words and some don't.

5. The art in picture books doesn't have to be drawings or paintings.

6. Picture books are a new idea that was invented in this century.

7. Sometimes picture books can be made into TV shows or films.

8. Just as a movie can win an Academy Award, a picture book can win a prize.

9. Because picture books have only a few pages, they can be written and illustrated in just a day or two.

★PICTURE BOOK QUIZ ANSWERS★

1. FALSE. It's true that most books for babies are picture books. But lots of great picture books have been written for older kids. There are even some picture books that adults enjoy.

2. FALSE. Most picture books have words and pictures, but some famous "wordless" books tell stories using just pictures. A famous example is Raymond Briggs' *The Snowman*.

3. FALSE. While many picture books star make-believe characters, others feature ordinary people, celebrities, heroes from the past, nature, or just about anything else you can think of.

4. TRUE. Sometimes authors tell their stories in rhyme, because readers enjoy that kind of writing. But lots of well-loved picture books are written in prose (non-rhyming sentences).

5. TRUE. Besides drawings and paintings, the art can be torn-paper collages, woodcuts, linoleum prints, or photographs, as in *The Red Balloon*.

6. FALSE. Picture books have been around for a long time. One of the first, entitled Orbis Pictus, was written about 300 years ago.

7. TRUE. Some picture books that became movies are: *The Little Mermaid*, *Cinderella*, *Beauty and the Beast*, and *How the Grinch Stole Christmas*.

8. TRUE. The best-known American picture book prize is the Caldecott Medal, named for Randolph Caldecott, a picture book illustrator. Each year, since 1938, the American Library Association gives this prize to a book voted "best." Caldecott winners include: *Why Mosquitoes Buzz in People's Ears*, *The Ox-Cart Man*, *One Fine Day*, and *Where the Wild Things Are*.

9. FALSE. Making a picture book involves many steps. Some writers take days, weeks, or months working out the stories. Deciding how the pages should look and then creating eye-pleasing art can also be a long-lasting job.

★UNDERSTAND THE STEPS★

Some authors write quickly. Others write slowly. Whatever the speed, most follow the steps shown here.

1. Get an idea for a story. Because ideas can come at any time, many authors keep pencil and paper handy. They write down ideas even if they don't know how the stories will end.

2. Play with the story idea. Try to create a mental movie. This means seeing the action in your head. Imagine different characters and try out all sorts of endings. You might make a simple outline. It will list the most important actions. This kind of outline is like a human skeleton. The whole body is not there, but you can see the shape and where the parts go. The outline helps the author tell the story in a way that makes sense.

3. Write a first ("rough") draft. The goal is to get the basic story written. Don't worry about making everything perfect. You may think up new ideas for the story, or dream up an ending that you hadn't thought of before.

4. Revise the first draft. The author reads the rough draft and makes changes which "polish" the story. These changes may be small, like adding or leaving out a word. Or the changes may involve a lot of work, for example, creating a new scene or moving parts around.

★UNDERSTAND THE STEPS★

5. Design the layout. This means planning the look of the pages. Designing a book calls for answering many questions. Will there be one big picture on a page or many little pictures? Will the pictures be drawings or photos? Will the pictures go above the words, under the words, or next to the words?

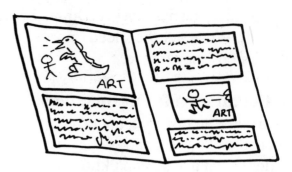

6. Create the art. Artists usually draw in pencil first so they can easily make changes. These pencil drawings are called "roughs." They don't have to be perfect. But they should show what the art will look like on the page. Later, the artist will redraw the roughs in ink, watercolor, or other art materials.

7. Letter the words. Some books are hand-lettered. However, most are typeset using computers. There are hundreds of different kinds of type, from fancy to simple. Type also comes in many sizes.

8. Paste up the pages. Putting the words and art together is called "paste up." This can be done by pasting or gluing the words and pictures onto pieces of cardboard, or it can be done with a computer and other machines.

9. Bind the pages. The pasted-up pages are called "camera ready." This means that they can be photographed, and then copied many times. The pages, along with a cover, are then combined into a single book by sewing, stapling, or some other means of binding.

STUDY PICTURE BOOKS

Thousands of picture books have been published over the years. Each one is different, and yet most of them have a lot in common. Discovering the basic parts can help you get ready to write your own picture books.

Picture Book Study Questions

- Does the cover make you want to read the book?
- Who wrote the book?
- Who illustrated it? (Sometimes one person does both jobs.)
- When was the book published? (Look on the copyright page, which usually is the second page.)
- Was the book dedicated to anyone? A dedication is a note by the author to someone special. It usually appears on the second or third page.
- How many pages does the book have?
- Does every page have words?
- Are the pictures in color, black and white, or both?
- Is there information about the author and the illustrator? Look at the back of the book or on the book jacket flap.

Try this: *Find a picture book. Then answer the questions in the Picture Book Study Questions box.*

Bonus: *Browse through a library or bookstore. What kind of books catch your eye? Notice whether the title or the cover art gets your attention. Make a list of titles that you like. Write a quick description of book covers you find attractive.*

LEARN ABOUT AUTHORS

A good introduction to almost any activity is to study someone who knows how to do it. If you want to fly planes, learn about pilots. If you want to be an inventor, learn about inventors. And if you want to create picture books . . . you guessed it! Learn about picture book authors.

Try this: *Find a living picture book author to interview through the mail. (A librarian might help you find one.) Ask the author a few specific questions that you really want answered. Keep your letter short because most picture book authors are busy and get lots of mail. Send your letter to the author's publisher. Include a self-addressed stamped envelope.*

Bonus: *Visit a children's library and find books about authors. Look up your favorite author. See if you can find information about the author's education, hobbies, special skills, and so on.*

★A DAY IN THE LIFE★

Authors and illustrators don't just write and draw all the time. They talk on the phone, do research, write letters, eat lunch, buy materials, read, take breaks, and spend time with their families and friends. Here's a sample page from the daily log of Mike Artell, showing a typical day in the life of an author/illustrator.

NOVEMBER

OCTOBER 26

6:00 — Got up, dressed, ate breakfast
7:00 — Read newspaper - got 2 story ideas!
8:00 — Worked on "Space" book
9:00 — "   "   "   "
10:00 —   Took a break 10:40 - 11:00
11:00 — Called Ed. Drew roughs. Wrote letters.
12:00 — Lunch. Post office. Bank. Art Store.
1:00 — Library - Research on "space" book
2:00 — Answered mail. Returned phone calls.
3:00 — Worked on new book ideas. Took a break.
4:00 — Talked to publisher.
5:00 — Updated "Things to do" list. Cleaned drawing pens.
6:00 —

Show rocket stages in "space" book

PRACTICE READING ALOUD

Reading picture books aloud can help you become a better writer. Watch how listeners react to the words, characters, actions, and pictures. Look for ideas to use in your own books.

Try this: *Choose one or a few picture books that you like, and read them to a group of younger children. You might also test out stories, poems, or jokes that you've written.*

Read-Aloud Tips

1. Choose a book that fits your audience. Children get bored with books they don't understand. Check with a teacher or parent.

2. Practice reading the story and know how to pronounce all the words correctly.

3. Begin by sharing your opinion. You might say, "This is a very funny book." Or you could try a question such as, "Did you ever want an unusual pet? Here's a story about a pet shark."

4. Sit on the same level as your audience.

5. Read with energy. Change voices for different characters. Birds might have high voices. Bears might use low voices.

6. From time to time, look at your audience. Smile, look scared, or use other expressions.

7. Decide when to show the art. Sometimes it's best to show a picture before reading. Other times, do it while you read, or after you finish a page.

8. Stop to ask questions or explain words. Invite listeners to predict what will happen next.

Bonus: *Observe television news reporters. Study how they use their eyes to connect with the audience. Listen to the way they change tone for different kinds of stories.*

PART 2

GET IDEAS

PICK A SUBJECT

Almost anything can be the subject of a book. You can write about people, animals, places, things, ideas, feelings, dreams, games, or whatever else interests you.

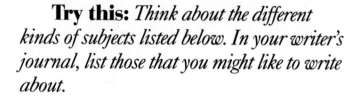

Try this: *Think about the different kinds of subjects listed below. In your writer's journal, list those that you might like to write about.*

Which subjects interest you?

- real animals?
- imaginary animals?
- yourself?
- people in your life—family, friends, neighbors, relatives, and so on?
- famous people—explorers, inventors, leaders, movie stars, sports stars, and so on?
- imaginary people—ghosts, robots, extra-terrestrials, and so on?
- funny happenings?
- scary things?
- faraway places?
- science?
- something else?

Bonus: *In your writer's journal make notes of things that interest you. These ideas may come from your daily life, from what you read or see on TV, or even from your dreams.*

★SUBJECT STARTERS★

If you can't think of a good subject for a story, try one of these:

Accidents • Acrobatics • Acting • Adults • Africa • Alligators • Ambulances • America • Amusement parks • Anger • Ants • Apes • Arguments • Armies • Art • Asia • Astronomy • Australia • Autos • Babies • Baking • Ball games • Balloons • Bare feet • Baths • Beaches • Beauty • Bees • Beggars • Being adopted • Being alone • Big things • Bikes • Binoculars • Birds • Blindness • Blisters • Bones • Boredom • Borrowing • Braces on teeth • Bravery • Bubbles • Busy people • Camping • Canada • Cats • Cavities • Chores • Church • Circuses • Clothes • Cold things • Cooking • Cousins • Cowboys and cowgirls • Cracks in the sidewalk • Crossing streets • Crying • Cuts • Dancing • Danger • Dark places • Days of the week • Death • Decisions • Democracy • Diamonds • Dinosaurs • Dirt • Eating • Ecology • Eggs • Electricity • Elves • Embarrassing moments • Emergencies • Escapes • Exercises • Family • Farming • Fears • Feelings • Fire • Fishing • Fixing things • Flags • Food • Football • Free things • Friendship • The future • Gadgets • Games • Garbage • Gifts • Golden Rule • Grandparents • Guessing • Gum • Habits • Hair • Heavy things • Helicopters • Heroes • Hiding places • Hiking • Hobbies • Holidays • Home • Honesty • Illnesses • Jack-o'-lanterns • Jet planes • Jobs • Jokes • Juggling • Jumping rope • Junk • Kaleidoscopes • Keys • Kissing • Kites • Lakes • Laws • Luck • Machines • Magic • Magnets • Mail • Making things • Malls • Manners • Maps • Marbles • Masks • Meanies • Medicine • Mexico • Mistakes • Money • Moon • Mud • Music • Neighbors • Nightmares • Noise • Numbers • Oatmeal • Oceans • Opinions • Opposites • Painting • Parades • Parks • Pets • Photos • Places you've been • Prizes • Puppets • Quicksand • Rabbits • Rainbows • Rainy days • Reading • Robots • Rockets • School • Science • Seasons • Shadows • Shopping • Slides • Snow • Spider webs • Stamps • Stars • Storms • Submarines • Swimming • Talk • Telephones • Telescopes • Thunder • Time • Tiny things • Toys • Tree houses • Tricks • Trucks • TV • Twins • Valentines • Voices • Volcanoes • Waiting in line • Whales • Wheelchairs • Wild things • Winning a million dollars • Zoos

WATCH REAL PEOPLE

Many picture books are about things that real people do: taking a trip, learning to ride a bike, getting lost, and so on. That's why you can get many story ideas by observing people all around you. Notice how they tease each other, walk, talk, work, do chores, play games, and relax. Often something that seems ordinary to the person doing it can lead to a really interesting story.

Try this: *Take a pad and a pencil to the playground or to the mall. Pick out a person and watch him or her for ten minutes. If possible, don't let the person notice that you are watching. You might pretend to be looking in a different direction. Make notes about the person's actions and appearance.*

Bonus: *What do you think someone would notice first about you if the person had never met you before? Write a description of yourself from that person's point of view.*

★PEOPLE-WATCHING TIPS★

1. Pay attention to people's faces. Their expressions can tell you what they are thinking or feeling.

2. Pay attention to body language. Watch what people do with their hands. Watch their posture.

3. Notice how people dress. Can you tell who's rich and who's poor? What clues do you see?

4. In a group, is a person quiet or talkative? Pay attention to how other members of the group treat this person and each other.

5. Notice if people appear to be in a hurry or not. See if you can tell by actions alone whether people feel at ease or nervous.

6. Be aware of the first thing you notice about individuals. When writing a story, you often want to focus on a character's most notable quality.

TELL A PERSONAL STORY

Many authors write about their own experiences. Because people are different, even stories about the same subject—for example, a trip on an airplane—can be original. The trick is using your firsthand knowledge, what you see and what you feel about the event.

Try this: *Choose an emotion that you felt recently, for example, excitement or fear. Write a few sentences that show what led to that emotion. Feelings are a good starting place for stories because everyone feels things differently.*

Think about a time you felt . . .

- angry
- bored
- confused
- excited
- frustrated
- happy
- lonely
- loving
- proud
- sad
- silly
- surprised
- thankful
- worried

What happened to make you feel that way?

Bonus: *Emotions are an important part of everyday life. In your writer's journal, keep track of all the different feelings you have in a single day. Add a line that explains what made you feel sad, happy, or whatever.*

TELL AN IMAGINARY STORY

Some stories are about make-believe characters or things. An example would be a tale about three-headed creatures living on a polka-dot planet where the favorite food is mud.

Try this: *Choose one imaginary story idea in the box—or think up one of your own. Then write a story about what would happen if that make-believe person or thing suddenly appeared in your life.*

Imaginary-Story Ideas

Characters who could:
    read minds
    be invisible
    stretch like rubber
    eat something unusual
    make music without an instrument
    talk to animals

Household objects that could:
    talk
    do chores
    duplicate themselves
    help with homework
    play games
    make up stories

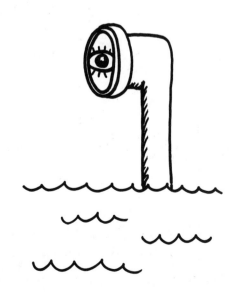

Bonus: *Create a fictional story about your future. It could be about an activity you've never done but want to do (like sky diving or traveling in a submarine). It could be about a real place you'd like to visit (Timbuktu or Mars). Before writing, gather the facts. This is called "research." Authors often do it by reading books, talking to experts, or looking at movies or videotapes.*

COLLECT WORD SOUNDS

Most books don't actually make sounds. However, authors often include "sound" words, such as bang, crash, meow, and sizzle. This way readers can "hear" the sounds of a story in their heads.

Try this: *Find sound words to describe the events in the box below or find examples from your own life. Begin by using sound words that are in the dictionary. Then try to make up brand-new ones.*

Sample Sounds

- shutting a car door
- egg breaking on the floor
- jet airplane taking off
- car making a fast stop
- baseball hitting a bat
- someone drinking water
- teeth being brushed
- tearing a piece of paper
- munching on potato chips
- jumping into a swimming pool
- a telephone ringing
- other happenings in your life

Bonus: *Using sound words is called onomatopoeia. Pick a sound word that you really like—for example, sploosh or boing—and write a few sentences in which that sound plays an important part.*

HOW TO CREATE PICTURE BOOKS

ASK "WHAT IF...?"

Many authors use a simple trick to discover exciting ideas. They take what's in front of them and ask, "What if...?"

Try this: *Choose a familiar story. It could be a fable, a nursery rhyme, a movie, or a fairy tale. Ask as many "What if" questions as you can about the story. For example, "What if Cinderella was a Native American?" Or "What if Cinderella got lost on the way to the ball?" Or "What if the Prince had caught up with Cinderella when she was running away at the stroke of midnight?" Give quick answers to the questions. Then choose the answer you like best, and turn it into a whole story.*

Playing with Who, What, When, Where, Why, How

One way to dream up a great story idea is to take a familiar happening and change one part of it.

For example, every day you have breakfast. The story is "What I Eat for Breakfast." Change the "who." Now you could have "What the President Eats for Breakfast."

Change the "what" and you could have "My Silliest Midnight Snack." Change the "when" and "who" and you get "What Kids Will Eat for Breakfast in the Year 2020." Add "why" and the story could be, "I Eat to Be Smart." Think about "how" and your story is "Twenty Ways to Make a Messy Breakfast."

Bonus: *Use the "What if...?" trick with your own life. For example, ask yourself, "What if I could turn myself into any animal?" Or "What if I were ten years older?" Or "What if I found out that my best friend was really from another planet?" Choose the answer to one of these questions as the starting point for a neat story about... you!*

INVENT CHARACTERS

Characters carry out the action in a story. Characters can be people, animals, or things (like robots) that act like people. When describing a character, it's best to focus on just two or three important facts. For example, you might have a character who is brave, bilingual, and handy with machines.

Try this: *Create a character using one or more methods in the Create-a-Character box. Then write a story starring that character.*

Create-a-Character Tricks

Personify: Treat an animal or an object as if it were a human being. An example would be a talking donut.

Combine: Turn two people into one character. For example, maybe you have a tall friend who plays the banjo. Another friend is short and does magic tricks. Your character could be a tall, banjo-playing magician.

Exaggerate: For example, if someone you know has a good memory, create a character who never, ever forgets anything.

Reverse: Change a quality into its opposite. For example, how about a gentle wolf or a scary lamb or a baby that talks like an adult or an airline pilot who's afraid of heights.

Bonus: *Turn yourself into a character. You might combine yourself with another person (or an animal!), or reverse one of your qualities. Try writing a story about the new you.*

★OUTRAGEOUS CHARACTERS★

✔ IDEA CHECKLIST ✔

Step 1. Review your writer's journal. Read and think about the subjects you've written about.

Step 2. Make a list of several subjects that really interest you.

Step 3. Choose your favorite subject.

Step 4. List the characters who will appear in a story that deals with the subject you've chosen.

Step 5. Decide what you want your story to accomplish:
- scare readers
- make readers laugh
- teach a lesson
- share an experience
- something else

HOW TO CREATE PICTURE BOOKS

PART 3

WRITE YOUR STORY

KNOW ABOUT PLOTS

Every story has a plot. It tells a story's main events in order. Here's the plot of "Goldilocks and the Three Bears":

Goldilocks enters the bears' home when they are gone. She eats their food, breaks things, and falls asleep. The bears return and scare Goldilocks away.

Before writing a story, an author may sum up the plot in a few sentences to organize the details of a story.

Try this: *Write the plot of a fairy tale, book, or movie. Use only a few sentences. Focus on the story's main events.*

The Soccer Star

People tell Tamika that she is too small to be good at sports.

Maria moves into Tamika's neighborhood and teaches her how to play soccer.

Tamika practices every day and she gets better and better.

Bonus: *Pick an important event from your life, for example, moving to a new home or learning to swim. Treat the event as if it were a story. Write a plot summary of it in three or four sentences.*

HOW TO CREATE PICTURE BOOKS

★SURE-FIRE PLOTS★

Journey: The hero travels to another place. The character may be lost, or trying to find the way home, or just searching for adventure.

Fight: Someone is trying to boss or hurt the hero. Often the hero is the "underdog." This means that at the beginning, the troublemaker seems stronger.

Escape: The hero has been captured and is struggling to regain freedom. The story usually involves several attempts at escape.

Quest: The hero is trying to find something valuable or rescue someone. In some stories, the hero learns an important truth about himself or herself, for example, that he or she can solve problems.

Comedy of Errors: A simple problem or situation gets out of hand, causing more and more problems. Funny things begin to happen. Often, the real solution is obvious and simple.

Learning a Lesson: The hero is warned of danger, but goes ahead anyway. Pride keeps him or her from admitting the mistake until it's almost too late.

★INSTANT PLOT PLANNER★

Here's a fun (and fast) way to create plots. The idea is to combine characters, actions, and places in unexpected ways. Sometimes the results are very funny.

Start by labeling three columns "WHO," "IS DOING WHAT," "WHERE." In the "WHO" column, list people and animals. For example:

WHO	IS DOING WHAT	WHERE
My teacher		
A cat		
An astronaut		

Now, without thinking about the "WHO" column, think of some action words and phrases—whatever characters might do. Write these phrases in the column titled "IS DOING WHAT."

WHO	IS DOING WHAT	WHERE
My teacher	is skateboarding	
A cat	is talking on the telephone	
An astronaut	is singing	

Now, without thinking about the first two columns, list places and scenes in the "WHERE" column. They can be big places, like another planet, or little places, like a baby's bed.

WHO	IS DOING WHAT	WHERE
My teacher	is skateboarding	at the mall
A cat	is talking on the telephone	in a tree
An astronaut	is singing	in the bathtub

Now, choose one item from each column. For example, "A cat is talking on the telephone in a tree." Why is the cat up in the tree? Who would the cat be calling? What's going to happen next? Think about several possible endings. Add more items under each heading and create more plots.

HOW TO CREATE PICTURE BOOKS

WRITE A WORKING TITLE

One way to plan a story is to think up a "working title." This kind of title uses one or a few words to focus on the story's big idea. A working title can help a writer stay on track while writing. Later, the writer may change the title to make it better fit the finished story.

Try this: *Choose an event. It can be real or imaginary. Write five or six working titles that might help you plan a story about the event. From this group of titles, pick your favorite. What makes it the best?*

Tips for Titles

- Be as specific as possible. For example, instead of "My House," you might try "The Third House from the Corner" or "A House Made of Stone."
- When brainstorming titles, use different forms of writing, such as questions and statements.
- Focus on the most important character or action. For example, if the story is about someone who gets lost, try using lost in the title.

Bonus: *At the library, look through lots of picture books. Write down four or five titles that catch your attention. Try to figure out what makes these titles special.*

BRAINSTORM SCENES

Brainstorming means getting lots of ideas fast. This kind of quick thinking is very helpful for thinking up *scenes*. These are little stories that happen within the big story.

For example, suppose your main idea is that the hero meets a talking cat. Brainstorming can help you turn that one idea into a rich story. For example, you might brainstorm scenes in which the hero and the cat:

- go shopping
- appear on a TV quiz program
- go to school
- save people in a burning house

Try this: *Brainstorm a list of scenes that might fit into a story about a character who can read minds.*

Hints for Brainstorming

Brainstorming has many uses. Before naming a character, an author may list many names to choose from. The same trick works for inventing titles. Some brainstorming tips are:

- Write your ideas as fast as possible.
- Include everything that comes to your mind. Sometimes silly thoughts lead to very useful ideas.
- Don't worry about spelling or neatness while you brainstorm.
- Push yourself. After you think you have run out of ideas, see if you can get at least one more.

Bonus: *Look through a picture book that you've read. Brainstorm other scene ideas that might have been in the story. Try changing something about a character or a place or a thing. After brainstorming a list of possible ideas, you might write your version of the book.*

KNOW WHO'S TALKING

Before writing your story, you must choose the narrator. The narrator is the voice that tells the story. There are three kinds of narrators:

- First-person narrators use "I" or "we."
- Second-person narrators use "you."
- Third-person narrators use "he," "she," "it," or "they."

Try this: *Retell a third-person fairy tale or other story in the first person. For example, you might begin "Jack and Jill" this way:*

Hi. My name is Jill. Jack and I needed to get some water for our family, so we took a pail and . . . .

Three Ways to Tell the Same Story

First person
We were walking along the beach when suddenly we saw a boat that looked like it was going to sink.

Second person
You were walking along the beach when suddenly you saw a boat that looked like it was going to sink.

Third person
Sandy and Tyler were walking along the beach when suddenly they saw a boat that looked like it was going to sink.

Bonus: *Describe an event in your life, but use the third person. For example, if your name is Nestor, instead of writing:*

I went to the dentist yesterday. I had a toothache.

your story might begin like this:

Nestor went to the dentist yesterday. He had a toothache.

MAKE AN OUTLINE

Before writing a story, an author may make an outline. An outline lists what happens in the story step by step. When writing the actual story, the author may keep the outline close by and use it as a guide to keep the story on track.

Try this: *For practice, write the outline of an event in your life, or of a story that you read or saw. Describe each important action in a short phrase or sentence. Number each step in the outline. See the sample in the box.*

Start of "Jack and the Beanstalk" Outline

1. Jack and his mother are happy, but poor.

2. Jack's mother tells him to sell their cow.

3. On the way to the market, Jack meets a man who trades Jack five "magic" beans for the cow.

4. At home, Jack's mother gets angry because she thinks Jack made a bad trade.

5. Jack's mother throws the beans out the window.

Bonus: *Take something with a simple shape, such as a key or your hand. Trace the object on a sheet of paper. Look at the outline. Even though you can't see all the details, you can tell a lot about the object. That's what an outline does for a writer. It gives a basic "shape" to the story. The details come later.*

HOW TO CREATE PICTURE BOOKS

★PICTURE OUTLINES★

Pictures help many people understand things better. If that's true for you, try planning your stories with pictures. Draw a picture for each scene. You don't need to make detailed drawings. Stick figures and scribbled backgrounds will do. You might add a few words to help tell what's going on.

The pictures below outline the first scenes of a picture book called *Jason and the Spaceship*.

JASON IS WALKING TO SCHOOL ONE DAY.

HE HEARS A FUNNY NOISE. HE LOOKS UP.

HE SEES A SPACE SHIP LANDING IN A NEARBY FIELD.

HE WALKS UP TO THE SHIP. THE DOOR ON THE SIDE OPENS SLOWLY.

Hint: *Here's a simple way to practice making picture outlines. Next time you're watching TV, pay close attention to a commercial that interests you. Then create a picture outline for the commercial.*

CHOOSE THE FORM

You can write picture books in prose or in rhyme.

Prose is everyday language. It's the way you talk when you tell someone what you did yesterday. Prose is written sentence by sentence. The sentences make up paragraphs. This paragraph, which is about prose, has five sentences.

Rhyme is told line by line. A word at the end of one line sounds like a word at the end of another line:

I think that I shall never see
A poem lovely as a tree.

While most picture books are written in prose, some famous ones, such as *The Cat in the Hat*, are told in rhyme.

Try this: *Rewrite the following rhymed story in prose. It's O.K. to use more words and different words.*

Zach and Bo

Everybody knew about the bully they called Zach.
He'd take a kid's lunch and then go and push him on his back.

One day the teacher said, "You'll all be pleased to know
That we have a brand-new student and his friends all call him Bo."

As soon as class was over, mean old Zach walked up to Bo,
And said, "You better understand, kid, I'm the one who runs this show."

And Bo just smiled at Zach and he said, "Nope. Not any more.
'Cause I've studied karate since I was only four.

"I don't believe in picking fights, but Zach, if I were you,
I'd try to make some friends because your bully days are through."

Bonus: *Style is how words are used. Some writers use as few words as possible to describe things. Others pile on words. Some use short words, others long words. One way to study style is to compare books on the same subject, for example, trucks. Read the books aloud to hear the different styles.*

BEGIN WITH A BANG

It's important to capture a reader's attention as soon as possible. Authors often do this by putting something exciting early in the story. A character might take a wrong path, make an important decision, or learn a secret.

Try this: *For each sentence below, think up a sentence or two that might build readers' interest. Don't write all the details. Just describe what could happen next to make the reader want to keep reading.*

Story 1. I woke up and went to the window. Suddenly . . .

Story 2. We had been driving for about an hour when up ahead we saw . . .

Story 3. The bell rang and the students entered the school. They came to their room, opened the door, and . . .

Some Story-Starting Surprises

It's surprising when a character:
- makes a big mistake
- meets someone scary
- gets lost
- breaks something
- finds something
- hears a weird noise
- gets into a fight
- sees something strange
- is faced with a life-or-death situation

Bonus: *Think about a time in your life when something unusual happened. Describe this happening as if it were a story. If you can't think of such an event, choose an ordinary activity and make up a surprise that could be the trigger for a thrilling story.*

WRITE A DRAFT

After you have a plot and an idea for an exciting opening scene, you're ready to write the actual story. This is called writing a first draft. As you work, you will describe:

- **Settings:** places where actions happen.
- **Characters:** people or creatures the story is about.
- **Actions:** what happens.

You will also write dialogue, the words characters say. Quotation marks (" ") surround these words.

Try this: *Write a draft of a picture book story. It could be made up, or it could be about a real event in your life. Include descriptions of settings, characters, actions, and dialogue. Be brief. Most picture books contain between 150 and 400 words.*

Bonus: *Choose a few picture books. Look for examples of each kind of description: settings, characters, actions, and dialogue.*

★SAMPLE FIRST DRAFT★

The first version of a story is called the "first draft." It's usually written quickly. The goal is to get all the parts onto paper or onto a computer screen. Then the writer can see what works and what needs to be improved. Many writers make notes to themselves on the first draft. They use these notes to make the next draft better.

Here's a draft for a picture book titled *The Backward Day*.

Too many "I's"

The Backward Day

change to third person

Last week I had a backward day. I was lying in my bed dreaming and slowly my eyes began to open until I was wide awake. I turned on the lamp and climbed out of bed. Next, I went into the living room where Mom and Dad were watching TV. I kissed them both goodnight and then went to the bathroom to brush my teeth. Then I got myself a snack and sat down to watch TV. When I was finished doing that, I went to take a bath. I took my bath and then put on my jeans and T-shirt. After my bath, Mom checked my homework; then I sat down to do my homework.

Change story to make child suddenly realize things are backward

TEST YOUR WORK

Many authors like to "test" their first drafts on readers. One way to do this is to give someone the draft. Another method is to read the story aloud while an audience listens. This way, the author can see right away how people react to the story. Do they laugh in the right places? Can they follow the plot? Do they have any questions or suggestions?

Try this: *Share a first draft of one of your stories with a few people. Before you read it aloud, explain to the audience that this is a first draft. Tell them that you are really interested in learning how they feel about the story. You might want to write down what the people say. You can decide later if you want to use their ideas.*

How to Choose a Test Audience

1. Choose people of different ages: adults, young children, and older children.

2. Make sure the audience contains boys and girls.

3. Choose people who will tell you the truth about what they think of your story.

4. Choose people who like to read, and who like good books.

Bonus: *Be willing to act as a "test reader" for other writers. When you give suggestions, you'll learn a lot about what goes into a good story.*

IMPROVE THE STORY

After testing a story, you may want to make some changes. You may decide to add a scene. You might change some words to make a description clearer or more exciting. This is the time to pay attention to every detail.

Try this: *Read the following sentences aloud. How many problems can you spot? On your own paper, rewrite the sentences in a better way. Be sure to check the spelling, too.*

First Draft Sentences

1. "What's wrong?", said the frog. "I'm very, very, very scared","," said the parrot. "Dont worry", said frog. "Why?", said the parot. "Because I'm sure we'll get out","," said the frog.

2. It was hot. Pablo looked around. He saw lots of stuff. He liked the desert.

Story Improvement Checklist

- All words are spelled correctly.
- All punctuation is correct.
- Sentences are different lengths.
- The same words aren't used over and over.
- Sentences make sense and are easy to read.
- The wording is clear. Exact words are used instead of ones like "thing."
- There aren't extra or missing words.

Bonus: *Read a few pages from a favorite book. Notice the words the author uses. Think about changes you might make if you had written this book.*

✔ WRITING CHECKLIST ✔

Step 1. Write a plot summary of your story.

Step 2. Write a working title that tells the main idea.

Step 3. Brainstorm interesting scenes for the story.

Step 4. Make a word or picture outline.

Step 5. Decide whether to use first person (I), second person (you), or third person (he or she).

Step 6. Decide whether to write your story in prose or in rhyme.

Step 7. Think up a first scene that will capture your readers' attention.

Step 8. Draft your story. Let the words flow out. Mix in dialogue for variety and excitement.

Step 9. Share your first draft with a trial audience. Ask for ideas about how the story can be made better.

Step 10. Polish your draft. Add missing details. Take away parts you don't need. Check the sentences, the spelling, and the punctuation.

PART 4

DESIGN THE BOOK

MAKE IT SPECIAL

Books that look interesting attract readers. The size and shape of the book are important. So is the art on the cover. Lettering also makes a difference—for example, should the words go above or below the pictures? Color can also be very eye-catching. All these things together are called the "design" of the book.

Try this: *Go on a design scavenger hunt in the library's picture book section. In your journal, list the titles of the following books:*

- *a book taller than wide*
- *a square book*
- *a book whose cover has words that curve*
- *a book whose inside pages have lettering under the pictures*

Also, look for very unusual designs, for example, a book with a hole cut into its pages.

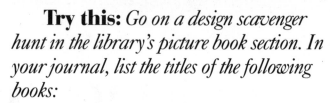

Bonus: *Get an idea for a picture book that could be in the shape of its subject. Possible topics include: cafeteria food, airplanes, computers, trees, clocks, shoes, and buildings. Draw an outline on a piece of paper or cardboard and then cut it out. Hint: Keep the shape simple.*

★ONE BOOK FOUR WAYS★

Differently designed books with the exact same content can have very different eye appeal. Here are four designs for a picture book.

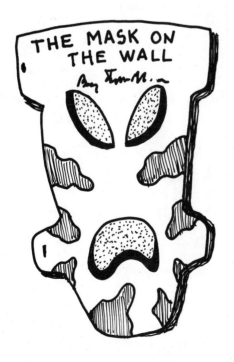

USE EYE-CATCHERS

Most picture books tell stories with just words and pictures. But some picture books also use special things known as eye-catchers to add interest and fun.

Try this: *Think up eye-catchers that might work with:*
- *a book about a furry kitten*
- *a book about soccer*
- *a book about a submarine*
- *a book about a garden*

Eye-Catching Ideas

- cotton, fabric, yarn, or other touchables glued to the pages

- cutouts of characters or scenes that "pop up" or "fold out"

- envelopes that contain letters, pictures, coins, maps, magnets, or other surprises

- flaps that open as doors

- wheels or clock hands that spin on rivets

- spaces for readers to glue in their own drawings or photos

- cut out "windows" that let readers look through one page to the next—often used to create a kind of guessing game

Bonus: *Choose a scene from a fairy tale, a nursery rhyme, or a story of your own. Create a page that uses an eye-catcher.*

★SAMPLE EYE-CATCHERS★

Cotton glued to page to make cloud and sheep's body

Fabric glued to page to make quilt

Envelope containing map glued to last page

Flaps taped or glued to page

★SAMPLE EYE-CATCHERS★

CLOCK WITH
MOVABLE HANDS

PLACES FOR
AUTHOR TO
PASTE PERSONAL
PHOTOS AND
DRAWINGS

PASTE PHOTO HERE

PASTE DRAWING HERE

POP-UP

WRITE AN ART MANUSCRIPT

Most picture books contain words and art. The art can be drawings, paintings, or photographs.

Almost always, the words come first. Then the artist, who might also be the writer, makes a list of the pictures that help tell the story. This list is called the "art manuscript."

The picture list can be written on a separate piece of paper, or it can be written in the margin next to the story.

Try this: *Choose a picture book and list the pictures in it. Use a few words or a sentence to describe each picture.*

Art Manuscript

Page number   Art
1   Cabin in woods
2   close up of Beth
3   Beth and pet cat
4   cat on rug
5   open window
6   view of cabin from outside
7   cat on path in woods
8   close up of scared cat
9   Beth walking into cabin
10   Beth running out of cabin
11   Cat sleeping in tree
12   Beth looking at cat in tree

Bonus: *Have someone read you a picture book without showing you the pictures. As you listen, sketch or write down ideas for pictures that might go on each page. Later, compare your art ideas with those used in the actual book.*

PLAN YOUR LAYOUTS

In a picture book, a page can contain just words, just art, or both. You must decide what to put on each page, and where the words and art should go. This is called making a "layout."

A layout is like a map. Simple sketches stand for the real art. Instead of printing letters, squiggly lines can show where the words will go in the finished book.

Try this: *Study five or six picture books. Look for the following layout patterns:*
- *a page with just art*
- *a page with just words*
- *a page with words above the art*
- *a page with words under the art*
- *a page with words next to the art*
- *two facing pages that share one piece of art (this is called a "spread")*

Bonus: *Plan a picture book using the words from a popular rhyme, such as "Twinkle, Twinkle, Little Star," "Humpty Dumpty," or "Mary Had a Little Lamb." Or use a poem of your own. Draw layout sketches to show how the words and pictures will fit together on each page.*

★SAMPLE LAYOUTS★

Top half of page is art. Bottom half of page is text.

←

Two or more drawings on a page with words in between

→

Words on the left page, art on the right page

↘

✔ BOOK DESIGN CHECKLIST ✔

The following steps should be taken after you have written a story.

Step 1. Decide how big your book will be.

Step 2. Pick a shape. Hint: While odd-shaped books can be fun, a book with square corners will be much easier to put together.

Step 3. Decide whether or not your book will include eye-catchers.

Step 4. Decide how many pages your book will have. Most professional picture books have 32 pages.

Step 5. Write an art manuscript. It should list all the pictures you want to include.

Step 6. Plan your page layouts. Sketch where the art and the words will go. You may wish to bind these sketches into a "dummy" book to see how the story flows.

PART 5

CREATE THE ART

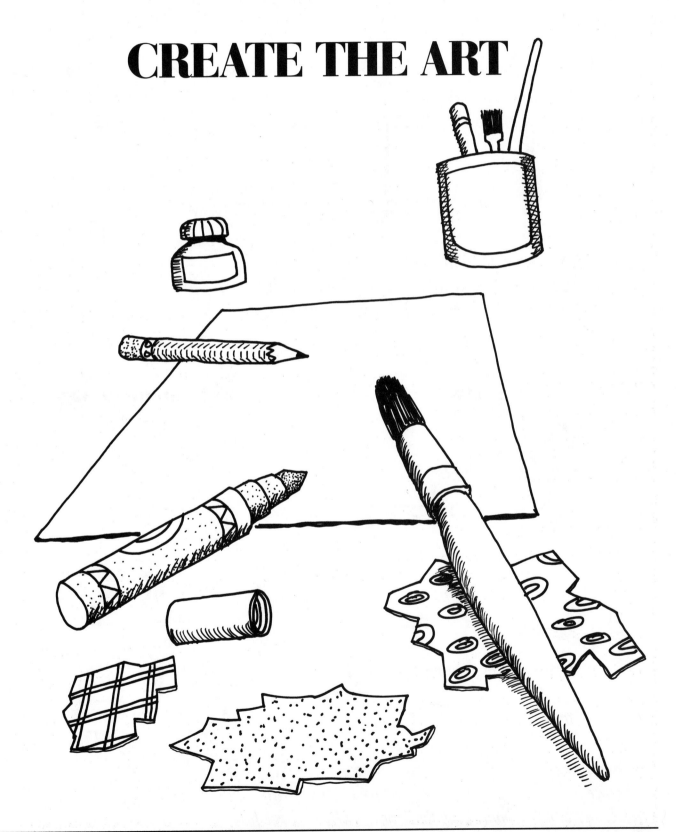

DRAW CREATIVELY

There are lots of ways to draw an object. You may sometimes need to try several versions before picking the one that looks just right.

Regular   **Thick Line**   **Nervous Line**   **3/4 View**

Try this: *Study the four boat pictures below. Then on another piece of paper, make four drawings showing different views of a single object, for example, a tree, a house, or a truck. The more you practice drawing, the better you'll get.*

A boat on a calm sea

A boat coming toward you

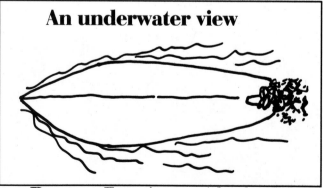

An underwater view

Looking out a porthole

Bonus: *Experiment with color. Draw a simple picture, then trace it four times. Color each picture in a very different way. Don't worry about using the "right" colors. Have fun.*

★DRAWING TIPS★

1. Draw in pencil first. It's easier to correct mistakes or change a drawing if you use a pencil first.

2. Sketch first, add details later. Sketch the characters, objects, and background quickly. Later, go back and "clean up" your drawing by adding details to clothing and faces, and erasing extra lines.

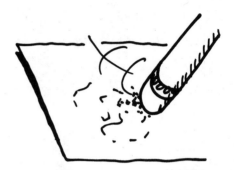

3. Erase gently. It's easy to tear or wrinkle your paper if you erase too hard. Try erasing in one direction rather than going back and forth. Work slowly, and you'll end up with a drawing to be proud of.

4. Think about ink. Some pencil drawings look better when traced in ink. If you use ink, let it dry, then erase all the pencil lines before you add color.

5. Add colors carefully. Some markers and watercolors "bleed" through paper and may give results you're not expecting. Experiment on scrap paper before you add color.

6. Let it dry. Pages must be completely dry before you move them. Otherwise, you might mess up a good drawing.

DRAW FROM LIFE

Artists often take a sketch pad and look for real things to draw. This helps them see things as they really are. It also makes drawings more accurate. Even artists who illustrate fantasy stories may wish to include pictures that look real.

Try this: *From memory, draw three familiar objects, for example, a tree, a fork, and a pencil. Next, draw the same three things while looking at them. Were you surprised by how many details you saw when you were drawing from life?*

Tips for Drawing from Life

1. If you're drawing plants and trees, notice how many different shades of green you see. Some parts of the plant will be darker green; others may be almost yellow.

2. Study textures. Does an object's surface look rough or smooth? Does it have a pattern? Draw what you see.

3. When drawing people, watch how they hold their bodies. Most people don't stand or sit perfectly straight. They lean, slouch, or bend a little at the waist.

4. Draw a little more quickly than you usually do. This will help you to notice the most important things first.

Bonus: *For one week, carry a small pad and a pencil around with you everywhere you go. Whenever you see something interesting, make a quick sketch of it.*

CHANGE YOUR VIEWPOINT

As you move from place to place, you get different views of the same thing. This is called "changing your viewpoint." For instance, a car tire looks different from the front than from the side. And if you come near it, you notice a pattern that isn't visible from far away.

Artists will often change the way they look at something so that they can draw it from a surprising angle. This can add interest, and also give new information about the subject.

Try this: *Take a sheet of construction paper or cardboard and cut a square hole in the middle of it. Make the hole about two inches on each side. Now look at an object through the hole. Move in close. Now move away. Move around the object. If possible, look down on it from above, and look up at it. Now draw the object from several points of view.*

Bonus: *Next time you watch TV, pay attention to the number of different points of view. You will see close-ups, long distance shots, and unusual camera angles (looking up and looking down).*

★DRAWING PARTS OF THINGS★

You don't always have to draw the entire subject. Sometimes it's more interesting to show a partial view. Here's an example:

In drawing 1 we see the whole person. In drawing 2 we see only the person's head and shoulders. Because we're closer to the subject, details are clearer. This kind of close-up also allows us to use bigger areas of color, which can have lots of eye appeal.

The same idea applies to objects. Compare the drawings below, and decide which would work better in a suspense book.

DANGER AT THE OLD MINE!

Hint: *Sometimes you'll want to draw two pictures of the same subject. The one that's farther away from the subject can set the scene. The close-up drawing can then show an important detail.*

TRY USING BORDERS

You don't need to use borders. But sometimes they help to keep drawings focused. Borders can be simple lines or repeating shapes and patterns.

Try this: *Cut a 7" by 9" (18 cm. x 23 cm.) piece of heavy construction paper or cardboard. Center it on a piece of unlined typing or computer paper. Now trace around the cardboard with a pencil, making a border on the unlined paper. Color the space between the border and the paper's edge. Draw a picture on the paper. Compare it to another drawing you've done without a border. Which do you like better?*

Bonus: *Study the sample borders in the box. Then think of other borders that would fit with your story. For instance, a border of wavy lines might be good for a story about the ocean. After making sketches, create your own design on a border "master." If you decide to frame some or all of the pages in your book, you can use a copy machine to make bordered pages.*

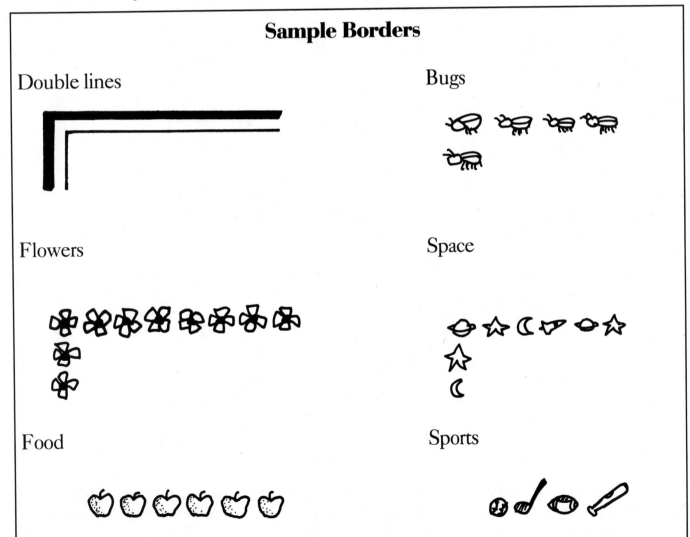

Sample Borders

Double lines

Bugs

Flowers

Space

Food

Sports

USE READY-MADE ART

You may need to draw a subject that you can't observe for real. It could happen if you are writing a story about camels and don't live near a zoo. The trick is to do research. Find a ready-made picture of your subject in a book or elsewhere. Study it as if you were looking at the real thing. Then make your own drawing of the subject.

Try this: *Practice drawing pictures using ready-made art. You can find pictures in many places: library books, magazines, newspapers, a family photo album, postcards, even drawings on food packages. You don't have to make an exact copy. You might experiment by changing the size or other details.*

Bonus: *Imagine that you're writing a picture book about a subject that you can't observe directly, and you want to show the subject on the cover of your book. Find a ready-made picture of the subject and make your own realistic drawing of it.*

★GALLERY OF READY-MADE ART★

FOR SCENERY

ENCYCLOPEDIA OPEN TO SECTION ON PYRAMIDS

PICTURE BOOK PAGE SHOWING PYRAMIDS WHICH AUTHOR HAS INCLUDED AS SCENERY

FOR CHARACTERS

MAMMALS

MAGAZINE WITH PICTURES OF MAMMALS

PICTURE BOOK PAGE SHOWING MAMMAL AS THE MAIN CHARACTER OF THE STORY

DRAW FROM IMAGINATION

Some stories are about imaginary things. Artists cannot draw these subjects from life, so they use their imagination.

Try this: *Imagine you're writing a book about a creature from another world. How could you make the creature as different as possible from humans? Ask yourself questions like:*

- *Will it have a head? How about two heads? Or three?*
- *Could an eye go on the nose?*
- *Could it have three mouths so it could talk, eat, and play the tuba at once?*
- *Could its body be square?*

When your imagination is working, sketch your creature from different angles and show it doing different things, as it might do in your story.

But what if everybody laughs?

Nobody wants to be laughed at. That's why some people never try to think up new ideas. But anyone who has ever tried to do something different has taken that chance. When you write and draw from imagination, you may create stories and pictures that other people don't understand. That's O.K. Even if some people laugh, others will like what you're doing. Keep using your imagination and thinking creatively. Before you know it, the people who used to laugh will be lining up to read your books.

Bonus: *Sketch an imaginary world. Start by changing a few basics. For example, what would the world be like if animals or babies were in charge, or if there were no gravity?*

HOW TO CREATE PICTURE BOOKS

★SECRETS FOR WILD ART★

Here are some tricks to experiment with.

1. Exaggerate: Try enlarging one part of your subject. What would happen if you made a cat's whiskers twice as big as they really are, or drew a person with feet as long as he or she is tall?

2. Simplify: Leaving out details can create an unexpected "look."

3. Anthropomorphize: This big word simply means making things look or act like people.

4. Make it move: Adding little curved "motion lines" and drawing your subject off the ground can make it look as if it's moving.

5. Use repetition: Drawing something once may not be too interesting, but drawing it many times (repetition) can make readers look twice.

ADD PERSONALITY

Authors develop characters with words. Artists use drawings to do the same thing. Characters with lots of personality are more interesting and fun to read about.

Try this: *The characters on this page each have their own personality. On a separate piece of paper, create characters that have other kinds of personalities. Examples might include timid, worried, or hard-working. Remember, your characters don't have to be people. They can be animals or even objects.*

Bonus: *Think about one or two people you know who have very strong personalities. Try using their personalities in the next story or book you write.*

INCLUDE BACKGROUNDS

Even good drawings of characters look plain without backgrounds. Backgrounds help the reader get a feel for the surroundings in which the action is taking place. Backgrounds can be outdoor scenes or the insides of places, such as buildings or cars.

Try this: *Draw a character that you might want to use in a story. On two or three sheets of paper, draw several different backgrounds for the character. Include at least one indoor scene. With a pair of scissors, cut out your character and place him, her, or it on the different backgrounds. Does the character take on any new characteristics or qualities on each of the backgrounds?*

Bonus: *Walk around your house and neighborhood. Sketch some backgrounds that you might be able to use in a future story you write.*

CREATE THE FINAL ART

When you're happy with your sketches, it's time to create the final art. This may be done by tracing the sketch or by redrawing it freehand. Don't try to do too much at one time. Take breaks and let your hands and eyes rest.

Try this: *Choose one of your pencil sketches and trace over the lines in ink.*

Another method is to place a new piece of paper over the pencil sketch and trace the lines that come through. If you can't see the lines clearly, tape the sketch to a window.

Whichever method you use, make three copies. Color one drawing with markers, one with watercolors, and one with colored pencils. Which one do you like best?

Things to Know About Adding Color

1. Watercolors work best with special watercolor paper.

2. Watercolors take time to dry. Don't be impatient and mess up a great drawing. After your artwork dries, you can make the colors deeper by going over them again with the same markers or watercolors.

3. Some marker ink spreads out, and makes a thicker line than you expect. Also, colors can blend and go in the wrong places.

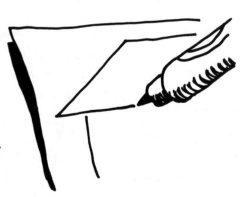

4. If your drawings are big and fairly simple, either watercolors or markers will work O.K. But if your drawings have a lot of detail, you might do better using colored pencils with sharp points.

5. If you create art using cut or torn pieces of paper, glue them on carefully so they don't stick to other pages.

Bonus: *Create a drawing using "mixed media."*
This means using more than one kind of coloring method.
Experiment with mixing watercolors, colored pencils, and crayons.

★SPECIAL EFFECTS★

Here's how to make drawings stand out:

- Use "puff paint" to give texture to drawings. Use "slick paint" for a wet or shiny look. Both kinds of paint are sold in craft shops.

- Glue colored felt to drawings to make fuzzy animals, leafy trees, and soft clouds.

- Drip alcohol onto a wet watercolor drawing to make the color spread in unusual ways.

- Drop a few grains of salt onto a wet watercolor drawing to soak up a little of the color. The result is usually very pleasing.

- Add a "pop up" figure on one or more pages to give readers a surprise. This is very useful in scary stories where things "jump out."

- Draw characters in silhouette. A silhouette is an outline drawing, filled in with a solid color.

- Sprinkle glitter on a thin layer of glue when you want to fill the sky with stars or if you want to show hot sparks coming from something such as a fire or an engine.

- Use wrapping paper or printed cloth for wallpaper and rugs when you're drawing a scene inside a house or building.

- Experiment with newsprint (old newspapers), tissues, and pieces of brown paper bag to create textures for clothing and other items.

✔ ART CHECKLIST ✔

Step 1. Read your manuscript and make a list of the pictures you want in your book. This is called an "art manuscript."

Step 2. Make a layout of each page, showing how big the art will be and where it will go. You don't have to write the actual words. You can just put in squiggles to stand for the words. (This is called "Greeking.")

Step 3. Make a sketch of the art you need for each page. Draw it to the size indicated in your layout.

Step 4. Read through the book, looking at each sketch in turn. As you read, you may get ideas for changing the art.

Step 5. Decide if you want the art to be in borders. If you do, create a master border page. Then make photocopies of it.

Step 6. Make the final black and white copies of each piece of art, either by tracing or by redrawing.

Step 7. Add color.

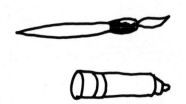

PART 6

PUBLISH THE BOOK

CREATE A GREAT COVER

Eye-catching covers, with interesting titles, attract readers. If the cover of a book is dull or uninteresting, the book may never be read. Think about the following as you work on your cover:

- Do you want one big picture or several small ones?
- Will the art fill the whole cover or just part of the space?
- What colors will work best?
- Where will the title go—at the top, in the middle, or at the bottom?

- Where will the author's name go?
- Do you need other words to invite readers inside?
- How big will the lettering be?

TITLE?

LETTERING?

THE DAY THE CAFETERIA FOOD CAME TO LIFE

By

COLORS?

AUTHOR'S NAME?

PICTURE?

ADD THE LETTERING

The words of your book may be hand-lettered, typed, or printed by computer. Lettering that's made with the help of a typewriter or computer is called "type." Lettering should be the same throughout the book. It should also be neat and easy to read.

Here are some words to know when you work on your lettering.

Case: Letters come in upper-case letters, also called "capitals"—
ABCDEFGHIJKLMNOPQRSTUVWXYZ
and lower-case letters—
abcdefghijklmnopqrstuvwxyz

Shape: A letter can have many shapes. You can have fun creating your own letters. Or, if you're using a computer, you can use ready-made letter shapes called "fonts." Two popular fonts are

"Courier"–
ABCDEFGHIJKLMNOPQRSTUVWXYZ
abcdefghijklmnopqrstuvwxyz

and "Times"—
ABCDEFGHIJKLMNOPQRSTUVWXYZ
abcdefghijklmnopqrstuvwxyz

Size: Letters come in many sizes, and are often measured in points—

Size (14 point)
Size (18 point)

Sometimes a large, upper-case letter is used at the beginning of a page or chapter. This is called an "initial cap"—

One day last spring, the sun smiled.

Weight: Letters can be plain or bold (printed dark) or *italic* (slanted).

WRITE A DEDICATION

Many authors include a dedication in the front of their books. A dedication is a personal note from the author to someone else or about someone else. Examples of dedications are:

- To my cousin Jennifer, who has always been my best friend.

- This book is dedicated to my crazy dog, Coconut.

- I dedicate this book to my teacher, Mrs. Hartman. Thanks for all your help.

- For my Mom and Dad, who encouraged me to write the best book I could.

Writing your book has taken a lot of time and effort. Think of three or four people who would appreciate all the work you've done. Write a dedication to each one. Hint: For more ideas about how to write a dedication, you might look at the dedications of several books from the library.

After you write your dedications, pick the one you like best, and include it in your book. Or include all of the dedications.

Front Matter

If you look at a few picture books, you will often find the following pages at the front of the book.

Title page: This is the first page. It contains the title of the book and tells who wrote and illustrated the book.

Copyright page: This contains the dedication, plus the year that the book was published and the name of the company that puts out the book.

Contents page: This lists the chapters that appear in the book. Most picture books don't have chapters, and therefore don't have contents pages. But if your book does have chapters, you might include a contents page to help readers see what's in the book.

Introduction: The introduction tells readers what's in the book and why the book is valuable. Most picture books don't have introductions, but some do. If there's a story behind your book—for example, a real event that gave you the idea—you might include an introduction.

BIND THE PAGES

After you combine your words and art onto separate pieces of paper, it's time to join these loose sheets into a book. First, you might want to glue the front and back cover sheets onto poster board or construction paper. This will keep the book from getting ragged.

Second, you might number each inside page. Most picture books don't have numbered pages, but some do.

Third, decide how many copies you'll want of your book. In the old days, books were copied by hand. You can still do it this way. But it's easier and quicker to use a photocopy machine. These machines can even copy pages back to back. This means that there will be no blank pages in the book. (You can create the same look by gluing pages back to back, but this can be messy.)

Now it's time to join (bind) the pages into a book. Books that you see in a bookstore or library are usually bound by giant machines that glue and press the pages together. Most copy stores can bind pages using simpler machines that join pages with pegs.

You can also bind your book by hand using a stapler or other easy-to-find tools and materials.

THREE WAYS TO BIND A BOOK

There are many ways to bind a book. Try one of the following methods or experiment with materials found at school or home.

Stapling

Simply line up the pages and carefully punch staples along the edge near the spine. If you're using cardboard front and back covers, you may need a heavy-duty stapler.

After the staples are firmly in place, cover them with a strip of cloth or plastic tape. This will help keep the staples in place, and will give the book a more finished look.

Ring Binding

Use a hole puncher to punch three holes along the edge near the spine. Then slip plastic or metal rings into the holes.

Yarn Binding

Use a hole puncher to punch six or more holes along the edge near the spine. Then use yarn or thick twine to "sew" the pages together. Be sure to tie a firm knot so that the pages will stay together.

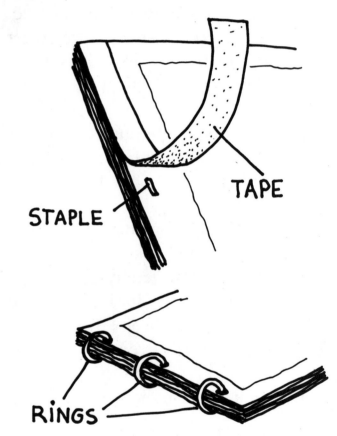

STAPLE

TAPE

RINGS

YARN

REVIEW YOUR BOOK

Congratulations! Your book is finished and you're just about to share it with lots of people. Take one last look. Are you proud of your work? You should be. You have created something brand new. This book did not exist until you created it.

Did you learn anything as you were writing and illustrating your book? Was it harder or easier than you thought it would be? What did you learn about yourself? Were you surprised at all the good ideas you had? When you started, did you think your book would end up looking this good?

If you're like most authors and artists, you probably see places where you could have made changes to make your book even better. That's normal. Keep these changes in mind (or better yet, write them down in a notebook) and use them the next time you create a book.

You've done a great job. Now that you know how to create picture books, what would you like to write about next?

SHARE YOUR BOOK

Unless you're writing a diary, you'll want to share your book with others. Here are a few ways to make sure people get to see and read your book:

- Give a copy to your local or school library. Ask the librarian to set up a special area for "kid-created books."

- Display your book at a local bookstore. Ask the owner for a special "kid-created book" area.

- Ask your doctor or dentist if you can leave a copy of your book in the waiting room for other kids to read.

- Give a copy to friends or relatives. They'll love it, especially if they are in the book or if they are familiar with the characters, scenes, or events.

- Read your book to a group of kids at story hour at your school or library.

- Enter your book in a Young Authors Contest.

- Sell copies of your book as a fund raiser for a club or organization.

- Put a copy of your book in a plastic bag and save it. Years from now, you may want to read it to your kids.

- Trade copies of your book with other kids who have written books of their own.

READING LIST

ART SKILLS

The Complete Crayon Book by Chester Jay Alkema (Sterling, 1969)

Copycat Drawing Book by Sally Kilroy (Dial, 1981)

Draw 50 Creepy Crawlies by Lee J. Ames with Ray Burns (Doubleday, 1991)

Drawing with Markers by Richard Welling (Watson-Guptill, 1974)

Ed Emberley's Big Green Drawing Book by Ed Emberley (Little, 1979)

Ed Emberley's Drawing Book: Make a World by Ed Emberley (Little, 1972)

How to Draw Lettering by Judy Tatchell and Carol Varley (Usborne, 1991)

How to Draw Monsters and Other Creatures by Cheryl Evans (Usborne, 1987)

I Can Draw It Myself by Dr. Seuss (Random House, 1987)

Let's Make Rabbits by Leo Lionni (Pantheon, 1982)

More Dinosaurs! by Michael Emberley (Little, 1983)

Pen and Ink by Don Bolognese (F. Watts, 1986)

SPECIAL FORMAT BOOKS

Cut-out and Window Books:

Joseph Had a Little Overcoat (It was full of holes) by Simms Taback (Random House, 1977)

Peek-a-boo! by Janet Ahlberg (Viking, 1981)

The Very Hungry Caterpillar by Eric Carle (Collins-World, 1969)

Watch Out! A Giant! by Eric Carle (Collins-World, 1978)

Envelope Book:

The Jolly Postman or Other People's Letters by Janet & Allan Ahlberg (Little, 1986)

Flap Book:

Where's Spot? by Eric Hill (Putnam's, 1980)

Moveable Books:

Lavinia's Cottage by John S. Goodall (Atheneum, 1983)

Barbara's Birthday by James Stevenson (Greenwillow, 1983)

Pop-up and Fold-out Books:

The Adventures of Paddy Pork by John S. Goodall (Harcourt, 1968)

House at Pooh Corner: A Pop-up Book by A. A. Milne (Dutton, 1986)

Madeline (pop-up book) by Ludwig Bemelmans (Viking, 1987)

The Most Amazing Hide and Seek Alphabet Book by Robert Crowther (Viking, 1978)

TEACHER TIPS

HOW TO CREATE PICTURE BOOKS offers step-by-step directions for learning or applying important creative skills. These include thinking, writing, designing, and illustrating.

You can easily tailor the material to fit students' needs. If children want help finding subjects to write about, you might begin with Part 2, "Get Ideas." For tips on turning ideas into stories, see Part 3, "Write Your Story."

With young children, you might present the lessons orally. Able readers can use photocopied pages to work independently or in small groups.

The following activities give other strategies for introducing and using the picture book format.

Read aloud picture books: Oral reading—by teacher or students—is a fine starting point for a picture book unit. Older students can gain valuable public-speaking practice by conducting story hours for younger children.

Vary selections in terms of content, form, and style. Page 77 of this book suggests examples of books that use eye-catching devices described on pages 46-48. The box on page 79 suggests several widely-available guides to picture books.

Ask a children's librarian to discuss picture books with your class: Librarians can enrich your program in many ways, for example, by telling about famous authors or by demonstrating book-binding tricks.

Publish a Class-written Book: Creating a picture book involves many skills. One way to give beginners an overview of the process is to produce a class book, with every child contributing a page or two. This whole-group effort can lead to individual or small-group projects. Examples of topics that work well for group-made picture books are:

Hiding Places
A Dream I Had
A Friend Is . . .
What Makes Me Smile
I Get Angry When . . .

An excellent model of this type of theme book is *Never Talk to Strangers* by Irma Joyce (Golden Press, 1971).

Invite local artists to share art techniques: While book illustration is a specialized field, it draws upon many basic design concepts. Even if you can't locate someone who illustrates picture books, you might find an artist to demonstrate drawing techniques, use of color, collage making, and so on. A field trip to an artist's studio might be a memorable experience. Hint: Your high school art department can be a rich source of guests. To a fourth grader, a high school artist may serve as an accomplished model.

Visit a local printing company that does color work: Your students might enjoy observing the steps that go into color printing and professional binding.

TEACHER TIPS

Relate picture books to the whole curriculum: In any subject area, students can create nonfiction picture books that package what they have learned for classmates or for younger children. Examples include:

- The Life Cycle of a Fly
- How to Use a Microscope
- Columbus' First Voyage
- What Makes a Rainbow

Celebrate students' achievements by sponsoring a "Young Authors Conference": Local or state reading associations often have information about organizing this kind of event. The typical elements include:

- An assembly featuring a picture book author who reads from his or her books, and offers insights into creating picture books. If you can't find a picture book author, try another type of writer or artist.
- A display of children's books in the library, the multipurpose room, and store windows around town. Invite parents and the community at large to read and enjoy the publications.
- Readings by young authors at story hours for younger children.
- A sale of books if students have made multiple copies. Receipts might be used to purchase materials for future publishing efforts—art supplies, a binding machine, a computer printer, and so on.

Ask your local newspaper's book reviewer to write an article about the conference and about the students' efforts.

Consider writing contests: While some teachers feel that contests over-emphasize competition, others find contests to be motivating. You might let students decide if they want to enter a contest. In any case, warn them that the odds of winning a top prize are slim.

A popular contest, open to elementary and secondary students, is "Written and Illustrated By . . ." The yearly deadline is May 1. For details, send a self-addressed business envelope, with two stamps, to:

Landmark Editions, Inc.
P.O. Box 4469
Kansas City, MO 64127

Have fun! It's more important for a child to enjoy the process of creating picture books than to produce a perfect book.

PICTURE BOOK GUIDES

A to Zoo: Subject Access to Children's Picture Books by Carolyn and John Lima (Bowker, updated regularly). Lists thousands of books by topics: aardvarks, friends, nightmares, sports, and so on.

Best Books for Children: Preschool Through the Middle Grades by John Gillespie and Christine Gilbert (Bowker, 1985).

The New York Times Parent's Guide to the Best Books for Children (Times Books, 1989).

Who's Who in Children's Books: A Treasury of the Familiar Characters of Childhood by Margery Fisher (Holt, 1975).

INDEX